ACE DEFENSEMEN

Jonathan Bliss

Rourke Book Company, Inc.
Vero Beach, Florida 32964

The Rourke Book Co., Inc.
P.O. Box 3328, Vero Beach, FL 32964

Bliss, Jonathan.
    Ace defensemen / by Jonathan Bliss.
        p.   cm. — (Hockey heroes)
    Includes bibliographical references and index.
    ISBN 1-55916-011-X
    1. Hockey players—Biography. 2. Hockey—Defense. I. Title. II. Series.
GV848.5.A1B54 1994
796.962'092'2—dc20
    [B]   93-38210
                                                                                      CIP
                                                                                        AC

Series Editor: Gregory Lee
Book design and production: The Creative Spark, San Clemente, CA
Cover photograph: Ken Levine/ALLSPORT

Printed in the USA

Contents

Defenders such as Calgary's Al MacInnis strive to keep the puck out of their zone and away from their goal.

Hockey on the Defensive

There are few positions in hockey that get less attention than the defenseman. The sports pages are filled with the exploits of wingers and centers because they score the points. Goalies also get praise because they stop the other team from scoring. But the defenseman is about as visible to most fans as the referee. You only know he's there when he isn't.

The defenseman's main duty is simple: to help his goalie protect the net. He can poke-check the puck away from a charging opponent, bodycheck an opponent into the boards, or hipcheck him to the ice. The defenseman can obstruct the flight of the puck by blocking it with his body, or he may, on certain occasions, foul the opponent. All of these activities require strength and quickness.

A great asset to the defenseman is speed—the more he has, the more things he can do on the ice. At the very least, he must have enough speed to cover his offensive counterparts, usually while skating backwards. Since exceptional speed is a rare commodity in any sport, two types of defensemen have developed: the physical defender, who stands his ground and will not be moved; and the speedy defenseman, who outmaneuvers and outruns his opponents.

Besides stopping the opposition forwards, defensemen usually start the play in the opposite direction by passing the puck to one of their forwards, or head-manning the puck into the opposition zone. But while they are frequently playmakers, good at setting up or passing the puck, few defensemen ever get the opportunity to become great scorers. Usually their offense is limited to power plays, when they can set up within their opponent's blue line and overwhelm the goalie.

Where a star center may get 30 to 60 goals a season, a top-flight defenseman normally scores only 10 to 20 goals at the most. Few defensemen have ever scored 100 points for a season, but it takes more than scoring to win a championship. It takes solid defense. The most consistently successful franchise in hockey, the Montreal Canadiens, did not win all their championships merely because they possessed great scoring forwards, but because they had great defensemen.

In the Beginning

The National Hockey Association was formed in the 1880s. This was an amateur league, which included several memorable teams like the Quebec Bulldogs, the Montreal Wanderers, the Montreal Victorias, the Ottawa Silver Seven, and the Montreal Shamrocks. In 1892, a man named P.D. Ross got the bright idea of matching the two best teams in the league in a championship series at

Although Boston's Ray Bourque is a tireless defender, he is also an offensive threat every time he gets the puck.

the end of the season. The prize was a silver cup donated by Canada's Governor General, Frederick Arthur, better known by his English aristocratic title, Lord Stanley of Preston. Thus began the Stanley Cup Championships.

Some of the early star defensemen in the league included Harvey Pulford, Hod Stuart, Si Griffis, Jack Laviolette, and Joe Hall. Pulford was an all-around athlete, one of the best Canada ever saw. He was equally adept at football, lacrosse, boxing, rowing, paddling, and squash, winning championships in virtually every sport he tried. Hockey came just as naturally to him. He was a defensive standout for the Ottawa Silver Seven from 1893 to 1908 and played on three straight Stanley Cup winners. Pulford is best remembered for his clean but hard-hitting style that greatly contributed to Ottawa's Stanley Cup wins over Kenora and Dawson City.

Brothers Hod and Bruce Stuart are Hall of Famers. Hod was a defenseman, and joined the Ottawa Senators in the 1898-99 season. Over the next five years, he played for the Quebec Bulldogs, Calumet, and the Montreal Wanderers. With Stuart in defense, the Wanderers won the Stanley Cup in March, 1907. That summer, on June 23, 1907, Stuart was killed in a tragic diving accident. During his brief career, Hod scored a total of 16 goals in 33 games, establishing himself as the first great defenseman in hockey history.

Si Griffis was the star defenseman for the championship Kenora, Ontario team that won the Stanley Cup in 1906-07. Griffis started as a rover in the seven-man game but moved back to defenseman later on. His combination of quickness and intelligence made him one of the first true two-way hockey players (that is, he played both offense and defense). He was so highly respected at his position that the citizens of Kenora awarded him a gold purse filled with money and a fine home. But after 1907, Griffis retired to Vancouver where he remained until 1911, when he joined the Vancouver Millionaires and became their captain. On opening night, he played the full 60 minutes, scoring three goals and two assists. In 1915, Griffis led his team to the Stanley Cup. He remained with Vancouver through the 1918 season when he retired for good, becoming an outstanding golfer and pin bowler.

Jack LaViolette was a rare athlete, named to both the Hockey Hall of Fame and Canada's Sports Hall of Fame. A sportsman equally talented at lacrosse as hockey, LaViolette took advantage of his great speed to outposition and outmaneuver his opponents. Laviolette has also earned a place in the hearts of all hockey fans as one of the original founders of the Montreal Canadiens. He played point (defense) for Montreal, moving up later in his career to play forward on a line with Hall-of-Famers Didier Pitre and Newsy Lalonde. Laviolette played on the Stanley Cup-winning team in 1916 and retired the following year. In the summer of 1918, Laviolette lost a foot in an accident, but he returned a year later to do some refereeing.

A Tragic Hockey Year

Joe Hall was one of the first of a breed of hard-hitting defensemen. He played pro hockey for 14 years, starting with Kenora, then later with the Montreal Shamrocks, the Quebec Bulldogs (where he won the 1911 and 1913 Stanley Cups), and the Canadiens (winning the NHL title in 1919). Hall and the Canadiens moved on to face the Pacific Coast Hockey Association winners, Seattle, in the 1919 Stanley Cup. With the series tied 2-2-1, the championship series promised to be a nail-biting finish. Unfortunately, it was never played. The Department of Health had to cancel the remainder of play because of a worldwide influenza epidemic. More people died in that one year from influenza than had perished in the previous five years during World War I. One of the victims was Joe Hall, who died on April 5, 1919 cutting short a brilliant hockey career.

Eddie Gerard was a star football, paddling, cricket, tennis and lacrosse player, but turned to hockey in 1913 with the Ottawa Senators and became their captain by 1920. During the ten years he spent with the Senators, he played on four Stanley Cup winners. Known as a gentleman on and off the ice, he played defense cleanly, using his speed and intelligence rather than sheer brawn to thwart the opposition players. He retired from hockey in 1923 because of asthma and coached the Montreal Maroons, winning a Stanley Cup for that team in 1926.

Sprague Cleghorn was just the opposite of Eddie Gerard. Cleghorn was one of the roughest, toughest players hockey ever saw, playing defense for both the NHA and the NHL from 1911 through 1928. He played six seasons with the Montreal Wanderers, several more with the Ottawa Senators, then three more with the Boston Bruins. He started out as a forward for Renfrew in the NHA, but was moved back to defense to play alongside

Hockey fans will never know how great Joe Hall could have been. He died of influenza after playing for three Stanley Cup-winning teams.

defenseman-center-rover
Fred "Cyclone" Taylor. He
tried to emulate Taylor's
style using end-to-end
rushes to offset opponents.
In 17 years he scored 163
goals—surprising offensive
numbers for a defenseman
of the period—and played
on two Stanley Cup
winners (Ottawa in 1920
and the Canadiens in
1924). Cleghorn more than
most defensemen of his
period was a constant
threat to the opposition,
who could never afford to
turn their back on him.

*A born hockey star, Moose
Goheen played for the U.S.
Olympic team.*

Francis X. "Moose"
Goheen was born in
Minnesota, where he played defense for the St. Paul
Athletic Club team that won the McNaughton Trophy
twice at the U.S. Amateur championship (1916 and
1920). He fought in WWI and returned to play for St.
Paul. He was selected to the U.S. Olympic Team that
played in the 1920 Antwerp Olympics. When St. Paul
became a professional team, Goheen became a pro
hockey player. Goheen is known today primarily for two
reasons. First, he was one of the first players to wear
protective headgear. Second, although he was a
defenseman, his rink-length rushes made him a prolific
scorer, providing a model for many defensemen, like
Eddie Shore and King Clancy who followed him. They
used to call Moose the only "three-man rush in hockey."

The Maple Leafs of the early 1930s benefited from the outstanding defensive play of Frank "King" Clancy.

The First Superstars

During the 1930s the NHL began to encourage more offense, assuming that more scoring would mean more fans. Crowds always turned out for the great scorers. To improve conditions for scoring, the NHL slowly added new rules. Among the most significant were allowing the forward pass of the puck, a restriction on the number of players allowed in the defensive end (three including the goalie), and the creation of the red line to speed up the game and reduce the number of offside calls—a rule that is often cited as the beginning of hockey's modern era.

None of these rule changes made the defender's job any easier. In fact, it usually meant that the defenseman had to stay put in his own zone, and never get caught up ice. Only the quickest, most agile defensemen could risk entering

Defensemen Trivia

Q: Four rovers are in the Hall of Fame: Harry Westwick (1894-1907), Russell "Dubbie" Bowie (1899-1908), Frank Rankin (1906-14) and Fred "Steamer" Maxwell (1914-25). What is a rover?

A: A combination defenseman and forward, the rover was a position in the old seven-man hockey game. The rover was abolished by the NHA (the forerunner to the NHL) for the 1911-12 season.

the opponent's zone. On the other hand, by the 1930s and '40s hockey was attracting not only more fans, but also more athletes. The caliber of the players was improving and so, inevitably, were the defensemen.

King Clancy and Happy Day

Frank "King" Clancy was the NHL's first superstar defenseman. Not only was he a superior defender, he was also a formidable rusher and scorer. Clancy entered the NHL as a 150-pound teenager. Most rival defensemen outweighed him by at least 30 pounds, but Clancy made up for this lack with speed and agility. Despite his size, he never backed away from a fight, putting players around the league on notice that he could not be bullied or intimidated. He entered the NHL with the Ottawa Senators and soon became known for his two-way hockey. He spent 10 years with Ottawa, becoming the best defenseman in the league. Clancy's abilities came to the notice of Conn Smythe, owner of the Toronto Maple Leafs, who purchased Clancy's contract from Ottawa for the immense price of $35,000 plus two players—a record hockey transaction for those days.

Clancy was worth it. In his second year with the club (1931-32), Clancy helped lead the Maple Leafs to their first Stanley Cup. With Clarence "Happy" Day as his defensive linemate, Clancy led Toronto to two regular-season NHL titles before retiring in 1936. In his 16 years in hockey, Clancy scored 136 goals and assisted on 145 others—both outstanding figures for a defenseman of his era.

Clarence "Happy" Day was the other half of the King Clancy defensive line. Day spent 33 years in pro hockey, first as a player, later as a coach, referee, and general manager. Day joined the Maple Leafs in the late 1920s and was partnered with King Clancy in 1931,

14

forming one of the greatest defensive units of all time. Day was captain of the team that won the Stanley Cup in 1932. During the finals that year, Day scored three goals to put the Maple Leafs over the top.

Eddie Shore

In the estimation of many hockey purists, Eddie Shore (1924-40) is still considered the greatest defenseman ever to play hockey. During his 14-year career, Shore was known as the meanest defense-man in the league. His brand of hockey was simple: rough and tough. "The accent is on speed now," Shore said after his retirement. "I guess it's better for the fans, but I liked it better in the old days. Then it was pretty much a 50-50 proposition. You socked the other guy and the other guy socked you." This state-ment summed up

One of the early defenders who loved to play rough and tough was Eddie Shore of the Boston Bruins.

Shore's approach to the sport.

Shore joined the Boston Bruins and quickly became a fan favorite, infusing players and crowd alike with his winning spirit. His first year with the team, he helped Boston go from last place to first, and Boston went on to win the Stanley Cup. Ten years later, in

1938-39, Boston and Shore won the Cup again, this time with hot rookie goalie Frankie Brimsek between the pipes.

Bostonians who had previously only gone out to see the Red Sox suddenly found themselves pouring into Boston Gardens to see Shore lead the Bruins. When he had the puck, the whole crowd would be on its feet. As one reporter said: "When Shore carried the puck you were always sure something would happen. He would either end up bashing somebody, get into a fight, or score a goal."

Shore is the only defenseman ever to win the Hart Trophy for the league's Most Valuable Player four times (1933, '35, '36, and '38). He was also voted to the All-Star team eight times, and won two Stanley Cups.

Dit Clapper

Victor "Dit" Clapper's brilliant hockey career was no doubt helped by his linemate, Eddie Shore, but Clapper would have been a star anyway. Clapper was incredibly durable, becoming the first athlete to play in the NHL for 20 seasons, all of them with the same team: the Boston Bruins.

Clapper joined the Bruins in 1926 when he was 19 years old. He spent nine seasons at right wing and another 11 years as a defenseman. He became one of the top scoring players in the league. His second full season, Clapper helped the Bruins win the NHL regular-season title and the Stanley Cup. His next year, the Bruins finished first again and Clapper enjoyed his greatest season, finishing third in the league in scoring, with 41 goals and 20 assists in a 44-game season.

In 1937, Clapper returned to his old position at defense, joining with Shore to form one of the most feared defensive combinations of all time. He sparked the Bruins to four more league titles and two more

Stanley Cup championships before his career ended in 1947. That same year, Clapper was inducted into the Hall of Fame—the first man elected to the Hall while still playing! Clapper's career totals were 228 goals and 246 assists in 833 regular-season games. In 86 playoff games, Clapper gathered 13 goals and 17 assists. The result: three Stanley Cup championships.

"Black Jack" Stewart was known as a hard-checking opponent.

Rescue Ranger

From 1926 through 1938, Ivan "Ching" Johnson was one of the most colorful defensemen in the NHL. Johnson joined the New York Rangers at the age of 30, becoming a virtual one-man show on both offense and defense. His hard-hitting style resulted in many bruises for his opponents, but they also took their toll on him. During the course of his career, he broke a leg, a collarbone, and a jaw. Through all the cuts, bruises, and general mayhem, he always wore a smile, even when he was crushing an opponent to the ice. Both his skill and his smile paid off. The Rangers won their first Stanley Cup in 1927-28, followed five years later by a second. Johnson retired in 1938, and was inducted into the Hall of Fame in 1958.

"Black Jack" Stewart

To John Stewart, a bodycheck wasn't a weapon, it was an art form, and he did more to perfect that form than any other defenseman in NHL history. His coach at Detroit, Jack Adams, once said of him: "He was one of the strongest guys I've ever seen in a hockey uniform."

Stewart joined the Detroit Red Wings in 1938 and rapidly developed into a star performer. In 1942, he helped the Red Wings clinch the Stanley Cup and repeated the feat again in 1949. Over 565 games he only accounted for a total of 31 goals, plus five more in 80 playoff games. But scoring was not the skill for which Stewart was valued. His forte was hitting, pure and simple.

Several observers compared Stewart's physical style to Ching Johnson's—applying heavy bodychecks to forwards as they swept down into his wing. Like Eddie Shore, Stewart was also a good passer and could skate faster than most of his opponents gave him credit for. But the crowds came to see him check and block, to see him keep goals out of his own net. This he did superbly.

Red Kelly (in uniform) played every position in hockey except goalie. He helped the Toronto Maple Leafs win four Stanley Cups.

Red Kelly

Patrick "Red" Kelly played defenseman, center, and wing. But he broke into the league in 1947 as a defenseman, and it is at this position that he is usually remembered. A native of Toronto, his native team did not want him, so he joined the Detroit Red Wings at the age of 19. Kelly proved that the Maple Leafs made a mistake. In the 12-1/2 years he spent with Detroit, he established himself as the premier rushing defenseman in the league.

Kelly was a deft passer and an excellent playmaker. At the same time, he was no bruiser. In fact, he was one of the game's great gentlemen, winning the Lady Byng Trophy four times for his sportsmanlike play. Kelly defended his net with a combination of superior size and speed. He skated his position with such an economy of motion that nothing was wasted. He looked like he wasn't expending any energy at all out there, yet everyone on the ice and in the stands knew differently.

Kelly helped Detroit win eight regular season championships and four Stanley Cup titles. He was the first winner of the Norris Trophy (1954)—the league's award for the most outstanding defenseman. He was named to the All-Star team six times.

Ironically, Kelly moved back to his hometown and played seven seasons with the Maple Leafs, who finally recognized his talent. Toronto coach Punch Imlach converted Kelly to a center, and Kelly responded by becoming one of the league's best centers. Following his retirement, Kelly coached the Los Angeles Kings and the Pittsburgh Penguins.

Norris Trophy Hog

To be a great defenseman, you have to be the best skater and passer on the ice. You must be able to dominate play. No one fit this description any better than Doug Harvey. Between 1955 and 1962 he practically monopolized the Norris Trophy for the best NHL defenseman, winning it a record seven times. A left-handed shot, Harvey was an excellent blocker who had uncanny puck control. But his greatest talent came in controlling the pace of the game. Singlehandedly, Harvey could speed up or slow down the game. If the Canadiens wanted to kill time, Harvey brought the puck up ice slowly, maneuvering his way through forwards until he reached the blue line. Then he would weave back and forth along the line, sliding soft passes to teammates.

If, on the other hand, Montreal needed a quick score, Harvey would wind up in his own end and bring the puck up ice on an end-to-end rush, head-manning the puck into the defender's zone, stationing himself at the left point, passing off, always protecting against a possible breakaway by a rival player.

Harvey was the unchallenged leader of the Canadiens, the man who made the plays happen. Harvey led the Canadiens to five straight Stanley Cup championships from 1956 to 1960. During his 13 seasons with Montreal, he was named to the All-Star team 10 times. More of a playmaker than a scorer, Harvey never scored more than eight goals in a season, but he accumulated 452 assists. In the clubhouse as well as on the ice, Harvey was the team leader. He took this leadership to the next level by helping to found the NHL Players Association, a move that prompted angry management to trade him in 1961. Harvey became the player-coach for the New York Rangers, leading the lowly Rangers into the Stanley Cup playoffs for the first time in four years in 1961-62. That same season he won his seventh Norris Trophy and once again was named to the All-Star team.

Pierre Pilote

Pierre Pilote broke into the NHL in 1958 with the Chicago Black Hawks. A steady, hard-working defender, his style of play is best typified by the 1,353 penalty minutes he incurred during the course of his 14 years. But at the same time, Pilote was more than just a smasher, he was also a scorer, accumulating 559 points (88 goals, 471 assists) in his 976 games. While with the Black Hawks, he helped them win one Stanley Cup (1961) and earned himself eight All-Star appearances. During his first five years in Chicago, he never missed a game and was only forced out of the lineup by a shoulder separation in 1961. He was also rated the NHL's best defenseman three consecutive years (1963 to 1965). He played his final season in Toronto in 1968-69 and was elected to the Hall of Fame in 1975.

One of hockey's greatest players was not a winger or a center—it was defensemen Bobby Orr, a demon skater and scorer who was the city of Boston's most popular athlete.

Offensive Defensemen

By the 1960s, the NHL had finally decided to expand. From a central core of six teams, the league grew to two divisions and twelve teams by the 1967-68 season. The expansion did a lot to open up the game, and rule changes did even more. The increasing popularity of hockey assured the league of a steady stream of new and talented players for the future. As the league opened up, the opportunities for good players to get time on the ice increased. No longer would a potential star have to languish in the minors while waiting for his chance. More players were making their mark earlier in their careers in the expanded league. In addition, the basic philosophy of the game was changing. No longer were teams content to send their three forwards into the rival zone, leaving the defensemen back. The new game had lots of speed, better stickhandling, and more passing.

Few of these changes benefited the traditional defensemen. Like the goalie, he was confronted with a difficult situation: He was asked to guard against forwards streaking into his zone, unable to use the roughhouse tactics that had characterized Eddie Shore's and Ching Johnson's game in years past. The position called for a new breed of player. There was still room for the mean, tough fighter, but increasingly there was also a need for the fast and evasive defenseman who was as accurate with his shot as he was with his check.

Bobby Orr

Many fans believe that Bobby Orr was simply the greatest player ever to lace on skates. If he wasn't the greatest hockey player, he was certainly the greatest defensemen of all time. Certainly no one had greater natural gifts or a better work ethic than Orr. Square-jawed and muscular, Orr didn't carry an ounce of fat on his five-foot, eleven-inch frame. Add to that his extraordinary speed on the ice and his uncanny hockey sense, and you had the most formidable player of his era. As his friend and teammate, Phil Esposito, once said of Bobby: "All Bobby did was change the face of hockey all by himself."

Orr revolutionized the role of the defensemen in hockey. Prior to his appearance, defensemen stayed back in their own zone most of the time. Not Bobby Orr. He was so gifted, so much faster, that Orr became known for his end-to-end rushes. They were dramatic, breathtaking things. He would circle behind his own net, collect the puck with the nonchalance of a frog collecting a fly, then begin his rush. By the time an opponent realized what was happening, Orr was past him and bearing down on the goalie. If a defender tried to poke the puck away, Orr simply stickhandled away from him, or deked to either side. Once he closed in on the goalie, Orr would either feather a pass to Esposito, Hodge, or Bucyk in front of the net, or take the shot himself. He had a cannon for a slapshot, a wicked wristshot, and could thread the puck past a goalie no matter how little space there was.

As if his offensive prowess wasn't enough, Orr was also a great defenseman—equally adept at stealing the puck from a forward as he was at keeping it away from

24

rival defensemen. He could bodycheck with the best in the league and, when called on, could fight with the best of them as well. He was also an outstanding penalty killer—a player who must keep control of the puck when his team is short a man.

Orr signed a two-year contract with the Boston Bruins in 1967 at the age of 19. His first year Orr won the Calder Trophy as the top rookie in the league. As his coach, Harry Sinden, put it: "Bobby was a star from the moment they played the National Anthem in his first NHL game." Veteran defenseman and future Hall of Famer Harry Howell won the Norris Trophy that year and was delighted to get it. "I'm glad I won it now," Howell said, "because it's going to belong to Orr from now on." Howell's prediction was on the nose. Orr won the Norris Trophy eight straight years—a record never likely to be equalled—and in 1970 he became the first man in history to win four trophies in a single season: the Norris Trophy as top defenseman, the Art Ross Trophy for the top scoring title, the Hart Trophy as the league's most valuable player in the regular season, and the Conn Smythe Trophy as the MVP for the playoffs.

How did a defenseman win the Art Ross Trophy? It had never been done before, but the incredible Orr did it with ease, scoring 33 goals and 87 assists for 120 points. His nearest competitor for the scoring title was teammate Phil Esposito with 99 points. Not only did Orr win the title, he also scored more than 100 points—a record for defensemen. The following year, Orr did himself one better, scoring a blistering 37 goals and 102 assists (a league record) for 139 points. Only Esposito outpointed him with his magnificent totals of 76 goals and 76 assists for 152 points.

Orr and the potent Bruins won everything in sight in 1971-72. First, they took the regular season crown, then the Stanley Cup. For the third straight year,

*Seven-time All-Star Brad Park was a New York Rangers
mainstay at defense.*

Esposito and Orr were at the top of the scoring charts with Orr scoring 117 points to Esposito's 133. But even though Esposito beat out Orr for the scoring title, he couldn't break Orr's grip on the Hart Trophy for Most Valuable Player. Orr won it for the third straight year and also took the Norris for the fifth straight year. To add insult to injury, Orr once again won the Conn Smythe Trophy as the outstanding player in the playoffs.

During the 1974-75 season, Orr scored a career-high 46 goals and won his second scoring title with 135 points. He was also named to the All-Star team for the eighth consecutive year. Boston and the hockey world hoped Orr would never get old and most of him never did—all except his knees. Those were the weak links in the incredible force that was Bobby Orr. In 1976 on the eve of his sixth knee operation, Orr ended his 10-year association with the Bruins and became a free agent. Between operations he attempted a comeback with the Chicago Black Hawks, but his knees couldn't take it. On November 1, 1978, Bobby Orr retired. He was only 30 years old.

Despite a little over 11 seasons in the NHL, Orr held or shared 12 individual records. He tallied 270 goals and 915 points in only 657 games—a remarkable average of just under two points per game. He was voted into the Hockey Hall of Fame in 1979. Perhaps Orr's greatest honor came when the *Boston Globe* conducted a poll to determine that city's favorite athlete: It wasn't Ted Williams or Bob Cousy or Carl Yastrzemski or Bill Russell. The winner was Bobby Orr.

Brad Park

Brad Park had the misfortune to play defense at the same time as Bobby Orr. Had it not been for that, Park would certainly have been recognized as the finest defenseman of his time. Park was barely 20 when he joined the New York Rangers during the 1968-69 season. Early in his rookie year, he showed signs of what was to come when he assisted on four goals in one game against Pittsburgh.

Like Orr, Park was a highly mobile defenseman with great speed and a hard shot. Park was particularly dangerous on the power play when he set up at the point near the opponent's blue line, sending crisp passes to Jean Ratelle, Vic Hadfield, or Rod Gilbert in front of the crease, or hammering a slapshot through a thicket of legs into the net. His numbers reflected his scoring prowess, especially with New York in 1973-74, when he had 25 goals and 57 assists for 82 points.

Six years into a brilliant career, he was suddenly traded along with center Jean Ratelle for Phil Esposito and Carol Vadnais. In 1977-78, Park scored 79 points (22 goals and 57 assists) with the Bruins. On December 11, 1980, Park became only the second defenseman in NHL history to collect 500 assists. The first was Bobby Orr, who was Park's teammate briefly during the 1975-76 season. One can only imagine the terror defenders must have felt when confronting both Orr and Park on the same power play.

Unfortunately, Park shared another trait with Orr that would shorten his playing life: He was plagued throughout his career by knee and leg injuries. Park's knee problems followed him to Boston, and after a couple of surgeries he retired. Park was named to the All-Star team seven times. He appeared in the Stanley Cup playoffs for an amazing 17 consecutive years from 1969 to 1985.

Orr Breaker

If Bobby Orr and Brad Park were the great defensemen of the late 1960s and '70s, Denis Potvin was

Potvin's defensive play was a key to the Islanders' phenomenal success during the early '80s, when the New York team won the Stanley Cup four years in a row.

One of the most durable players in NHL history was Larry Robinson, who played more than 1,300 games for the Canadiens and the L.A. Kings.

one of the great defensemen of the 1980s. With the possible exception of Larry Robinson, nobody else was even in Potvin's class. He appeared in the New York Islanders training camp one day in autumn of 1973 as a 19-year-old, already endowed with a ready smile and extraordinary hockey skills.

Surely Potvin had all the potential in the world. Already he had smashed Bobby Orr's Ontario Hockey League records for a defenseman. Expectations ran high for the young man from Ottawa. But as Potvin himself said, "I'm not Bobby Orr and I know it. You can't compare us because our styles are different. I can't skate as well as Orr, but I feel there are a couple of things I might do better, like hitting." In fact, Potvin was a ferocious hitter. Potvin was a solid 205 pounds, with legs that kept him beautifully balanced on the ice, particularly when they were laying a body check on an unfortunate forward. His physical style of play earned him the fear of many players in the NHL, and his excellent passing made him the playmaker on the Islanders power plays.

Potvin scored 17 goals and 54 points in his first season, winning the Calder Trophy as the NHL's Rookie of the Year. Over the next 14 seasons, Potvin won the Norris Trophy three times and was a first-team All-Star five times. But Potvin will be chiefly remembered as captain of the New York Islanders. He was the point man and quarterback for one of the most consistent franchises in league history. Potvin was there along with Trottier, Bossy, Tonelli, Nystrom, and the rest of that team for four straight Stanley Cups from 1980 through 1983. By the time he retired in 1988 at the age of 34—after 15 seasons with the same team—Potvin had broken three of Orr's greatest records for a defenseman: most goals (310), most assists (742), and most career points (1,052).

Larry Robinson

Larry Robinson was born in 1951 some 30 miles from Ottawa, the birthplace of Denis Potvin. Robinson lacked Potvin's cockiness and was far more soft-spoken, yet he became the model for modern defensemen.

First off, Robinson was no shrimp. Like so many of today's defensemen, he was both big (212 pounds, six-feet, three-inches tall) and strong, yet he was also a fast skater who handled the puck well enough to be a forward (a position he played occasionally). Growing up on a farm had taught him the importance of hard work and, during his playing days, few men kept themselves in better condition than Robinson. He needed to: As a young player he made $60 a week with a Junior A team and had a family to support at the age of 19. He took a day job at a beverage company that paid him an additional $80 a week. He'd work all day, then lace up his skates at night for practice or games. It was this kind of dedication that led to his success in professional hockey.

Robinson was brought up to the majors by the Canadiens during the 1972-73 season. For the next 16 seasons, Robinson would be a mainstay of the team that became one of the greatest in Montreal and NHL history. His greatest offensive season came in 1976-77 when he scored 19 goals and 85 assists, won the Norris Trophy, and was named to the All-Star team for the first time. Robinson was also the league's Plus/Minus leader (an important indication of how successful he was at stopping goals at his end and scoring goals at the other end). A year later, he won the Conn Smythe Trophy as the MVP in the playoffs, scoring four goals and 17 assists in 15 games as Montreal won their first of four straight Stanley Cups.

Robinson won the Norris Trophy again in 1979-80. An outstanding blocker and pokechecker, Robinson's forte was strategy and positioning. He always seemed to set up exactly where the offense wanted to go and put his stick in the way of the puck a split second before it got there. He triggered the offense as well as anyone in the league, with an assortment of soft passes. He executed plays with workmanlike perfection, and had a menacing slapshot from the point on power plays. Unlike many other defensemen, Robinson always had more points on the score sheet than minutes in the penalty box. He could also kill penalties like few defensemen in history. With his long reach and good size, he could keep the puck away from opponents until they were nearly frantic.

This workhorse was signed as a free agent by the Los Angeles Kings for the 1989-90 season where he joined Wayne Gretzky and Luc Robitaille in making L.A. a big-time hockey town. In the three seasons he played there, Robinson became one of the fan favorites, winning his eighth appearance to the All-Star game in 1990-91. At the end of the 1991-92 season he retired, having compiled an impressive total for a defenseman: 208 goals and 750 assists in 1,384 games (ninth on the all-time NHL games played list). Even in his last season, Robinson was still enjoying the game. As he said himself: "This is too tough a game and too tough a league to play in if there isn't a little fun in it. Well, it's still fun for me."

Larry Robinson is second on the list of all-time assists leaders.

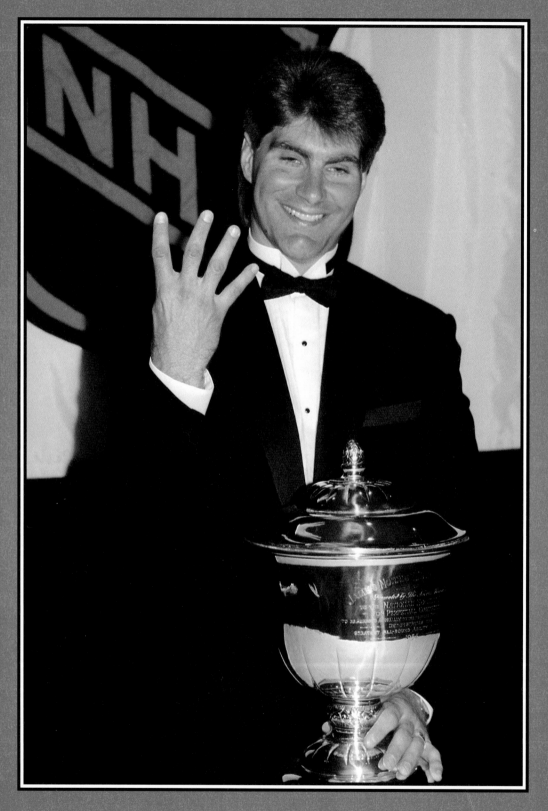

Ray Bourque is an outstanding scorer, winning four Norris Trophies.

Today's Stars

Hockey today is a far more sophisticated game than it was 20 or 30 years ago. First, the rules have encouraged more offense. Second, the increasing popularity of hockey has brought more big, talented players into the game. While there is still room for the small, speedy guy in hockey, the sport is increasingly becoming dominated by tall, rangy, muscular types with all the skills. Third, the game is played differently than it was a decade ago: The new approach emphasizes speed, passing, and teamwork. The game has been fundamentally changed by the introduction of the European hockey style which emphasizes speed and pinpoint passing. This new style was showcased by the Edmonton Oilers during the later 1980s when they

---

Defense Trivia

Q: Who was the only defenseman to ever win the Art Ross Trophy for the most points scored during the regular season?
A: Bobby Orr, who collected the trophy in 1970 and 1975.

Q: Four defensemen have won the Hart Trophy as the MVP in the league. Name them.
A: Eddie Shore (1935, 1936, and 1938), Ebbie Goodfellow (1940), Babe Pratt (1944), and Bobby Orr (1970, 1971, and 1972).

crushed opponents with their speed, passing, and playmaking to win the Stanley Cup five times in seven years.

While there are still Eddie Shore-type tough guys, defensemen nowadays must combine the defensive savvy of a Larry Robinson with the offensive threat of a Bobby Orr or a Brad Park in order to succeed in the league. Only a handful of the most talented defensemen in the league ever attain this. Here are a few of the best and brightest in today's NHL.

1,000 Games and Still Going

It wasn't enough that the Boston Bruins had Bobby Orr and Brad Park, they also had to get Ray Bourque as well. Not since Orr, perhaps, has a defenseman so thoroughly dominated his position as Bourque does. A lot has been expected of him ever since the Montreal native entered the Junior ranks.

The Boston news media hailed Bourque as the second coming of Orr, but that just wasn't so. For one thing, Bourque's game was subtler, more behind-the-scenes—unlike Orr's which was fast and flashy. But in another important respect, he showed the fans how right they were. In his first NHL game, Bourque scored a goal and two assists. That year he won the Calder Trophy for the league's best rookie. He was selected to the All-Star team—the only non-goalie ever to win both honors in a single year. From that point on he never missed an All-Star game.

Bourque's secret is his speed, his conditioning, and his work ethic. He frequently logs between 35 and 40 minutes a game, and seems blessed with the kind of physique and stamina that can handle the load. In his 14 years in the league, Bourque has always been near the top of the Plus/Minus stats, one of the more dependable indications of a defenseman's prowess.

Future Hall of Famer Ray Bourque has played more than 1,000 games—all for the Boston Bruins.

What makes Bourque a complete player is his offensive skills. Without seeming to, Bourque often finds his way to the front of the opponent's net at just the right moment to stuff the puck into the net or wristshot the puck by the goalie. Not that Bourque always looks to score. Like many great defensemen, he chooses his time. But when he decides to take the puck, there are few playmakers or shooters in the league that are any better.

Once in possession of the puck, it is very difficult to get it away from Bourque, especially after he builds up speed. Trying to knock him off the puck is almost impossible. As one of his coaches has said: "Ray is the best I've ever played with or seen on defense. Maybe Paul Coffey is more explosive offensively, but in a tight game, you couldn't ask for a better player."

During the 1982-83 season, Bourque led his team to the Adams Division and the overall point championship. He scored his best offensive year in 1983-84 when he tallied 31 goals and 65 assists for 96 points. In the 1986-87 season, he won the first of four Norris Trophies, scoring 23 goals and 72 assists for tenth place on the league's scoring list. Then in 1987-88, Bourque led his team to the Stanley Cup finals, scoring 81 points in the regular season (17 goals, 64 assists) and 21 points (three goals, 18 assists) in 23 games to earn his second Norris. Bourque was awarded back-to-back Norris Trophies in 1989-90 and 1990-91 for his continued excellent play.

Through the 1992-93 season, Bourque was still with Boston—14 years in the same uniform—and had accumulated more than 300 goals and 780 assists in more than 1,000 games. Surely, few players today are more likely to enter the Hall of Fame than Ray Bourque.

Offensive Dynamo

No defenseman has ever played offense the way Paul Coffey plays it—not even Bobby Orr. Like Orr,

Paul Coffey was part of the fabulous Edmonton Oilers team that won the Stanley Cup five times in one decade.

Coffey is blessed with blinding speed, remarkable moves, great stickhandling abilities, and an unfailing shot—all skills that contribute to his extraordinary statistics. In fact, Coffey is the only other defenseman besides Orr to contend for the NHL scoring lead.

    Coffey was drafted by the Edmonton Oilers in 1980. It was the beginning of a remarkable collaboration. He joined the likes of Wayne Gretzky, Mark Messier, Grant Fuhr, Jari Kurri, and Glenn Anderson to form one of the most talent-rich teams of all time.

Coffey's job was not only to anchor the defense, but to spearhead the offense. Taking a page out of Orr's book, Coffey would take the puck behind the Edmonton goal, then accelerate with a few effortless strides. By the time he reached the red line, most of the opposing players were struggling to keep up. Coffey would lead the charge into the opponent's end, or, with defensemen mustering in front of him, pass to the streaking Messier or Anderson coming down the middle.

How good is Coffey at what he does? In his second year with the Oilers, Coffey scored 89 points (29 goals and 60 assists) as Edmonton finished first in the Smythe Division and second overall in the NHL. The next year, Coffey scored 96 points. By the 1983-84 season, he was playing so well that he accumulated an incredible 126 points, including 40 goals and 86 assists, to become the second-leading scorer in the NHL. Not only did he win his third invitation to the All-Star game, he helped Edmonton win their first of five Stanley Cups, overwhelming the New York Islanders with offense.

Coffey and the Oilers won the Cup again in 1984-85 as he finished fifth in the NHL scoring race with 121 points (37 goals, 84 assists) and captured the Norris Trophy as the league's best defenseman. But his best offensive year was still ahead. In the 1985-86 season, Coffey scored 48 goals, snapping Orr's once untouchable record of 46 goals. He ended the season with 138 points; third overall in the NHL behind Gretzky and Mario Lemieux, and only one point shy of Orr's all-time record for a defenseman. Eight of Coffey's points came on March 14 when he tied the NHL mark for defensemen and equaled a backliner's record for assists in one game with six. He added still another record that year when he collected points in 28 consecutive games!

Coffey was traded before the start of the 1987-88 season to Pittsburgh. It turned out that Coffey still had someone to pass to: instead of Wayne Gretzky, he now had Mario Lemieux. With the same high-speed, highly-mobile offense that had typified the Oilers, Coffey fit right in. He scored 113 points in the 1988-89 season and 103 points in the next year. In 1990-91, not only did Coffey score 93 points for the Penguins, he also helped bring them their first Stanley Cup.

In 1991, the Penguins traded Coffey to Los Angeles where he was reunited with Jarri Kurri, Wayne Gretzky, Charley Huddy, and Marty McSorley on a revitalized King team. Unfortunately, he didn't stay long. After only part of 1992-93, Coffey was traded to the Detroit Red Wings where he continued to pile up impressive numbers, particularly when anchoring their power play.

Coffey remains one of the premier stars in the NHL and an ever-present threat on offense. In 14 NHL seasons, Coffey has accumulated more than 330 goals, 800 assists, and 1,100 points—all career records for a defenseman. He also holds the record for most goals, assists, and points by a defenseman in the playoffs.

Veteran Talents

The league brims with defensive talent. Many, like Rod Langway and Rob Ramage, have been around for some time. Others, like the precocious Alexei Zhitnik or Rob Blake, are just beginning to make their marks.

The veteran of NHL defensemen is Rod Langway. Langway and Larry Robinson went to the same school of defense. Both are six-feet, three-inches tall and well over 200 pounds. Both played for Montreal. Both are stay-at-home defensemen by design. Never a prolific scorer, Langway's major impact is on the other team's offense which he consistently stifles. Langway came up with the Canadiens during the 1978-79 season and stayed with Montreal for four years before being traded to the Washington Capitols where he still plays after more than a decade. His best years were 1982-83 and 1983-84 when he was awarded the Norris Trophy for the league's best defenseman.

Rob Ramage is in his sixteenth year in the league. During that time he has played for the Colorado Rockies, St. Louis, Calgary, Toronto, Minnesota, Tampa Bay, and Montreal. Known for his rugged play, Ramage has nonetheless contributed as a scorer, collecting 50 or more points four times. He has also been selected to four All-Star games and played on two Stanley Cup winners, the 1988-89 Flames and the 1992-93 Canadiens.

New Arrivals

Chris Chelios attended the University of Wisconsin where he anchored one of the best college teams in the country. He was one of the leaders of the upstart U.S. Olympic Hockey Team at the 1984 Games before joining the Montreal Canadiens. In 1984-85 he was selected to the NHL All-Rookie team while compiling an impressive 64 points. The next season he was part of the Stanley Cup-winning team, and in 1988-89 certified himself as one of the league's best defensemen by scoring 73 points during the regular season and 19 points in 23 games during the hard-fought playoffs (losing in the finals to Calgary). He was awarded the Norris Trophy for his efforts. Chelio was traded to Chicago for Denis Savard in the 1990-91 season, but his fine play continues.

Brian Leetch is one of the great young players in the league. While at Boston College the five-feet, eleven-inch Leetch won many impressive awards. He was also selected to the Hockey East All-Star Team and the NCAA East All-American Team. Leetch played for the U.S. in the 1988 Olympics and was then drafted by the New York Rangers.

Few defensemen score more than 70 points a season—few, that is, except Chris Chelios.

His college record was a good indication of the success that would follow. In his first year in the NHL, Leetch scored 71 points on 23 goals and 48 assists, winning the Calder Memorial Trophy as the NHL's outstanding rookie. Despite the Rangers quick exit from the playoffs, Leetch scored three goals and two assists in only four games. In 1990-91, Leetch scored 88 points on 16 goals and 72 assists. In 1991-92, he bettered this mark, scoring 102 points on 22 goals and 80 assists in winning the Norris Trophy. He enjoyed another outstanding playoff, scoring four goals and 11 assists in only 13 games.

Al MacInnis has played his whole career in Calgary and has helped lead the Flames to a Stanley Cup. Widely reputed to possess the hardest shot in the league, MacInnis has shattered several boards with his slapshot from the point and is feared by goaltenders throughout the NHL. An outstanding defender, he is a huge physical presence on the ice, equally capable of scoring or hitting.

MacInnis is also a consistent scorer, particularly on the power play. In 1988-89, MacInnis scored seven goals and 24 assists in 22 games, leading the Flames to the Stanley Cup. For this accomplishment he collected the Conn Smythe Trophy for the outstanding player during the playoffs. His best offensive year was 1990-91 when he scored 103 points on 28 goals and 75 assists.

Who are the rising stars in the league? Three of the best young defensemen in the league—Alexei Zhitnik, Darryl Sydor, and Rob Blake—play on the same team, the Los Angeles Kings. Alexei Zhitnik is an import from Kiev, Ukraine, where he helped win the 1990 Olympic gold medal for his country. He was drafted by Los Angeles and joined the team in the 1992-93 season, becoming both a brilliant defensive stopper and an offensive threat from the point with a looping, knuckleball of a slapshot that often beats goalies up high when they least expected it.

Rob Blake attended Bowling Green University. He entered the league in 1989-90 with the Kings, becoming one of the best stand-up defensemen in the league. Known primarily for his defense, Blake rarely misses a check and is strong enough to overcome most obstacles, such as forwards.

Obviously the NHL is suffering no lack of good defensemen. In fact, the quality seems better than ever before. No longer the forgotten man, defensemen like Bobby Orr and Paul Coffey have made this position as interesting to the fans as any on the ice.

Most Goals Made By a Defenseman

Name	Teams	Goals
Paul Coffey	Edmonton, Pittsburgh, L.A., Detroit	318 in 12 seasons
Denis Potvin	New York Islanders	310 in 15 seasons
Ray Bourque	Boston	272 in 13 seasons
Bobby Orr	Boston, Chicago	270 in 12 seasons
Doug Mohns	Boston, Chicago, Minnesota	248 in 22 seasons

Most Assists By a Defenseman

Name	Teams	Assists
Paul Coffey	Edmonton, Pittsburgh, L.A., Detroit	796 in 12 seasons
Larry Robinson	Montreal, L.A.	750 in 20 seasons
Ray Bourque	Boston	743 in 13 seasons
Denis Potvin	New York Islanders	742 in 15 seasons
Brad Park	N.Y. Rangers, Boston, Detroit	683 in 17 seasons

Most Points By a Defenseman

Name	Teams	Total Points
Paul Coffey	Edmonton, Pittsburgh, L.A., Detroit	1,114 in 12 seasons
Denis Potvin	N.Y. Islanders	1,052 in 15 seasons
Ray Bourque	Boston	1,015 in 13 seasons
Larry Robinson	Montreal, L.A.	958 in 20 seasons
Bobby Orr	Boston, Chicago	915 in 12 seasons

Plus/Minus Leaders for 1993-94

Name	Team & Position	+/- Rating
Scot Stevens	New Jersey - Defense	+53
Sergei Fedorov	Detroit - Center	+48
Nicklas Lindstrom	Detroit - Defense	+43
Frank Musil	Calgary - Defense	+38

Glossary

BODY CHECK. To use one's body to block an opponent. Legal only when the man hit has the puck or was the last player to have touched it.

DEFENDING ZONE. The area from a team's goal line to its blue line.

DEKE. To feint or shift an opponent out of position.

PENALTY-KILLER. A player whose job is to stop the opposing team when his team is one or two men short after a penalty is called. Once in possession of the puck, the penalty-killer tries to maintain control of the puck or shoot the puck down the ice.

POKECHECK. The quick thrust of a stick that takes a puck away from an opposing player. Usually done best by defensemen rather than forwards.

POWER PLAY. A manpower advantage resulting from a penalty to the opposing team.

SLOT. The area extending from in front of the net out about 30 feet. Many goals are scored from this area.

UP ICE. The other end of the rink.

Bibliography

Diamond, Dan and Joseph Romain. *Hockey Hall of Fame.*
New York, NY: Doubleday, 1988.
Diamond, Dan, ed. *National Hockey League 75th Anniversary Commemorative Book*. Toronto: McClellan & Stewart, 1993.
Hollander, Zander, ed. *The Complete Encyclopedia of Hockey.*
Detroit, MI: Visible Ink Press, 1993.
National Hockey League. *Official Guide & Record Book 1992-93.*
Toronto: NHL Publications, 1993.

Index